Executive Summary

In January 2005, veteran jihadi thinker, propagandist, and historian Abu Musa`b al-Suri released his 1,600 page study of the jihadi movement, *Da`wat al-muqawama al-Islamiyya al-`alamiyya* (*The Call for Global Islamic Resistance*). Suri hoped this book would stimulate the creation of a comprehensive jihadi curriculum for future generations of jihadi fighters, thinkers, and activists who could learn from the mistakes and successes of jihads past.

In *The Call*, Suri identifies twenty-five "paradigmatic jihadi movements," or particularly edifying historical cases, where jihadis have both succeeded and failed to rally supporters, defeat their opposition, or establish territorial control. However, many of these jihadi movients are very obscure, and, consequently rarely studied within the Western counterterrorism community.

In order to better appreciate the jihadi movement's strategic objectives and mindset, the Combating Terrorism Center at West Point invited David Cook, an expert on Islamic history and jihad, to provide deeper background on four of Suri's identified paradigmatic jihads:

1. The experience of the *Harakat al-Shabiba* in Morocco (1969)

2. The experience of the *Harakat al-Dawla al-Islamiyya* in Algeria (1982 – 1987)

3. The experience of the Afghani Arabs in Lebanon under Abu `A'isha al Lubnani

4. The experience of the Islamic Army of Aden Abyan in Yemen during the 1990s

Despite the factual errors Cook identifies throughout Suri's work, the latter's stature in the jihadi movement means that future jihadis will take his analysis seriously and model their strategies accordingly. Here are some of the most significant findings from Cook's survey:

1. **Yemen is a critical step in the jihadi march towards a global caliphate.**

    a. Suri and others believe that Yemen is ripe for a jihadi revolution because of the country's high levels of anti-American sentiment; its high rate of population growth; the high degree of weapon proliferation; and its proximity to the apostate regimes in Saudi Arabia and other Gulf states, as well as countries allied with the United States, including Ethiopia, Egypt, and Israel.

2. **The Sunni jihadi movement has gained little traction in Lebanon.**

    a. Suri is embarrassed by the fact that few Lebanese jihadis have been involved in the global movement (under 200 Lebanese came to fight against the Soviets in Afghanistan during the 1980s) and by the fact that jihadi groups have found little historical success in waging jihad in Lebanon, especially when compared to the success of Shia jihadi groups, primarily Hizb 'Allah. His lone paradigmatic jihad in Lebanon consists of a failed, obscure, and short-lived movement.

3. **Jihadi organizations should be global in their thinking but careful to build a broad constituency in their homeland.**

   a. Suri seems to favor those movements that, even if they found little success in reality, had the proper motives and methodology. The little-known *Harakat al-Shabiba* operating in Morocco in 1969, although considered even by Suri as ineffectual, embodies some the ideal characteristics of a jihadi group: it was inspired by the life and writings of Hassan al-Banna and Sayyid Qutb; focused on the youth, since they are not adherents of the political persuasions of previous generations (supporters of the Moroccan monarchy or advocates of Nasserite movements); sought to win the hearts of the underprivileged masses; and instigated a radical Islamic counter-society rather than conducting terrorist operations.

4. **Jihadis should not excommunicate other Muslims.**

   a. Suri argues that the slaughter of civilians by the GIA in Algeria from 1994-1998, which was legitimated by excommunicating them, was a colossal strategic error that should never be repeated. It is due to the rampant and public killing of Muslims by Muslims that, Suri contends, allowed the Algerian authorities to portray the radicals as barbaric, thereby causing the GIA to lose popular support and fracture.

DAVID COOK is an Assistant Professor of Religious Studies at Rice University. He is an expert in Islamic History, Muslim apocalyptic literature and movements, historical astronomy and Judeo-Arabic philosophy. David's most recent books are Understanding Jihad, and Contemporary Muslim. He is currently working on a book on the theme of Islamic martyrdom for Cambridge University Press, and has published on the subject of martyrdom operations.

JARRET BRACHMAN is the Director of Research at West Point's Combating Terrorism Center. He is specialist on the topics of *al-Qa'ida* strategy and use of new media technologies, particularly the Internet. He is currently managing several projects for different U.S. federal agencies concerning *al-Qa'ida* ideology and strategy.

CHRIS HEFFELFINGER is an independent terrorism analyst specializing in Islamic ideology and political affairs in the Middle East. He is the editor of *Unmasking Terror: A Global Review of Terrorist Activities, Volumes I* and *II*, with forewords by General William Odom (ret.) and Michael Scheuer, respectively. Mr. Heffelfinger has written regularly on terrorism issues, in particular covering jihadi ideology and the use of the web. He has also appeared in the media analyzing current events related to terrorism, most recently in the New York Times. He is currently a researcher for the Combating Terrorism Center at West Point where he works on issues related to Salafi ideology.

Paradigmatic Jihadi Movements

David Cook

THE EXPERIENCE OF THE *HARAKAT AL-SHABIBA* IN MOROCCO (1963= 1969)

1. Background

Abu Musa`b al-Suri in his *Da`wat al-muqawama al-Islamiyya al-`alamiyya* lists the "experience of the Harakat al-Shabiba" in Morocco as the first of his list of twenty-five paradigmatic *jihadi* experiences. This group, founded by al-Shaykh `Abd al-Karim Muti`,[1] is by far the most obscure of all the different groups listed by al-Suri, and seems to be the only one he is familiar with solely through book research. In his own words, he stumbled across the *jihadi* writings of Muti`, and also came across a history of the group which he had to leave behind when he left London hastily in 1997. He says that he was able to meet one of the members of the group who told him valuable details of its experience, but he does not remember them very well now. Significantly, he makes a number of mistakes in his short presentation concerning this group, including the actual date of its existence (1969, instead of the 1963 he lists).

The Haraka al-Shabiba (HS) or the Haraka al-Shabiba al-Islamiyya (The Organization of Islamic Youth), as it usually appears in works on the subject, was part of the turbulent political scene of Morocco during the 1960s and 1970s. For centuries Morocco had been ruled by the `Alawi dynasty, claiming descent from the Prophet Muhammad, which lent Islamic political legitimacy to the ruling elites. Although Morocco had been a French protectorate (1912-56) and had been the recipient of a large-scale French colonist movement, its struggle for liberation was no where near as traumatic as that of neighboring Algeria. Additionally, the Moroccan elites, while Frenchified, consistently led the struggle for independence and lost no legitimacy in the eyes of the people.

This sense of leadership was exemplified by the charismatic Muhammad V, whose exile at the hands of the French in 1953 led directly to the mass mobilization needed for independence. Muhammad V's return to Morocco in 1955 was a triumphant one, and the French gave up their protectorate soon thereafter. Thus, when Morocco achieved independence, its leadership was stable, the country more or less a homogenous population (most of the French colonists left, but those who stayed were welcomed as part of the society), and most importantly—as Muhammad V was part of the Prophet Muhammad's family—there was no significant Muslim opposition to his rule. Islam was obviously the basis for the society and, although there was a strong secular and left-wing element to Morocco, the revolutionary currents in Algeria and other places in Africa seemed to be ineffectual there.[2]

---

[1] Like all names in Arabic there are multiple spellings depending upon the system of transliteration used. Muti` is spelled Mottei or Mouti` in French language sources.

[2] See Holger Albrecht and Eva Wagner, "Autocrats and Islamists: Contenders and Containment in Egypt and Morocco," *Journal of North African Studies* 11:2 (2006), pp. 123-41; and M. Cooper, "The Islamic Movement of Morocco," *Arab Studies Journal* 1:1 (1993), pp. 4-52 for discussion.

2. History of the Haraka al-Shabiba

The rise of the Harakat al-Shabiba (HS) in the 1960s should be seen as part of the effort of the Moroccan authorities to counteract those left-wing trends, and especially the adulation of Egyptian President Jamal `Abd al-Nasir (d. 1970). Its founders, Muti` and Ibrahim Kamal, were both former teachers in the secondary educational system, and at least Muti` had apparently been associated with left-wing ideals during the early 1960s. But he had become disillusioned and left the educational system to found the Harakat al-Shabiba in 1969.

From the very beginning the group was focused for the most part on the youth that was less connected to the old order that largely supported the monarchy, or the left-wing labor or Nasserite movements. HS called for the establishment of a Muslim state and critiqued the old order for corruption, inability to maintain proper Islamic standards and excessively close relations with the U.S. and France. Apparently the source of Muti`'s radicalism was the writings of Sayyid Qutb, the Egyptian radical Muslim thinker who was executed by Nasir in 1966. Although Qutb's writings were banned in most of the Muslim world, they still circulated in some of the more conservative Arab monarchies (e.g., in Saudi Arabia and Jordan, and presumably in Syria) because the target of their critique was usually assumed to be Nasserism and more generally, the left. In Morocco at this time the monarchy was under some threat from these elements, and King Hasan II (1961-99) had to rely upon the army for support during the later 1960s and early 1970s because of his opponents' widespread popularity.

> "the Qutbian paradigm of a non-Muslim *jahili* society fit Morocco just as well as it did the more revolutionary regimes in Egypt and Syria..."

However, according to Muti` and his followers' analysis, the Qutbian paradigm of a non-Muslim *jahili* society fit Morocco just as well as it did the more revolutionary regimes in Egypt and Syria. Although Morocco was conservative and monarchical, it did not fully implement the *shari`a.* In addition to this issue, there were dramatic economic disparities that fueled HS's opposition to the monarchy. According to Muti`'s analysis, a truly Muslim state would not allow for the distinction between the king and his court's wealth as opposed to the poverty of the rest of the country.[3] And many of the youth who were drawn to HS came from the rural or lower classes who did not benefit from the stability of the state, which was the only group at that time that preached a revolutionary Islam.

HS was divided into two wings: the *da`wa* (proclamation) and *jihad* (fighting) sections. The *da`wa* section of the group was itself divided into five groups:

1. *shu`bat al-asatidha* (division for teachers)
2. *shu`bat al-mu`allamin* (division for scholars)
3. *shu`bat al-talamidh* (division for students)
4. *shu`bat al-`ummal* (division for workers)

---

[3] In 1970 Morocco's median income was the lowest of all of the North African states; see Park and Boum, *Historical Dictionary of Morocco* (Lanham, ML: Scarecrow Press, 2006), pp. 108-12.

5. *shu'bat al-hirafiyyin* (division for professionals)

Each one of these groups were further subdivided into *usar* (families), which in turn were headed by a *naqib* (deputy) who answered to the head of each division. The sum of all of the divisions formed the *shura* council of the *da'wa* section. This pyramidical organization, based upon that of the Muslim Brotherhood, was headed by Muti' himself.[4]

The organization reveals Muti''s own bias towards educational institutions as a basis for his movement, as well as his Marxist background. For a revolutionary organization, it is odd that there does not seem to be any section for the military. Other revolutionary Islamic organizations in Egypt and Pakistan were always very careful to penetrate the military, sometimes with spectacular results (as in the assassination of Sadat in 1981). Despite the devoted to the scholars, there does not seem to be any evidence that senior or junior *'ulama* were recruited into HS. Its primary membership was always drawn from students and displaced urban masses.

The *jihad* wing of HS was completely and hermetically sealed away from the *da'wa* section, and this fact makes some of the operations that were ascribed to HS problematic. It seems clear that a number of the more activist members of the group were placed in the *jihad* section which was either allowed to present itself a separate group or else Muti' was too weak to control this section of HS. Although the *jihad* wing of HS naturally attracted the most national attention, it was the popularity of HS among students that made the government suspicious of its intentions.

This suspicion was best reflected in the reaction towards Muti''s refusal to participate in the Green March of 1975, which King Hasan II had designed in order to boost his popularity. The Green March was a mass movement of Moroccans into the Western Sahara (then evacuated by the Spanish). All political parties were invited to join the Green March, and most accepted. But HS did not, claiming that the March was nothing but a maneuver to distract the population from Morocco's true issues. As a result of this unwillingness to participate in what the authorities viewed as a national enterprise (that even today commands wide support), it managed to insinuate a spy named Baha' al-Din al-Amiri into the councils of HS, and as he probed deeper into the true ideology of the group it became clearer that this was a revolutionary Islamic movement and not merely a buttress against the left as the Moroccan authorities had originally hoped.[5]

Consequently HS was banned and Muti' fled abroad (on Dec. 21, 1975), first to Iran, and then eventually to Belgium, with interludes in Libya and Saudi Arabia.[6] Activities

---

[4] Park and Boum, *Dictionary*, pp. 185-6; and see discussion in Faiz Sarah, *al-Haraka al-Islamiyya fi al-Maghrib al-'Arabi* (Beirut: Markaz al-Dirasat al-Astratajiyya wa-l-Buhuth wa-l-Tawthiq, 1995), pp. 49f.

[5] Park and Boum, *Dictionary*, p. 186; and Abderrahim Lamichichi, *Le Maghreb Face a l'Islamisme* (Paris: L'Harmattan, 1997), pp. 29-30; the group's account of al-Amiri is given in *al-Mu'amara 'ala al-Shabiba al-Islamiyya al-Maghribiyya: Khalfiyyat ightiyal Binjallun wa-l-watha'iq wa-murafa'at al-difa'* (Holland: al-Shabiba al-Islamiyya al-Maghribiyya, 1984), pp. 11f.

[6] It seems impossible to track his itinerary after leaving Morocco, see Henry Munson, *Religion and Power in Morocco* (New Haven: Yale University Press, 1993), pp. 160-1 (who says that he

of the group continued, including the violent assassinations and riots detailed below, but effectively Muti` was cut off from control of HS, and over the 1980s its activists splintered or trickled into other radical groups. Muti` himself was sentenced to multiple death sentences for murder *in absentia* and apparently has never been apprehended. His second-in-command, Kamal Ibrahim, never seems to have taken a leadership role; in the end HS was a one man show and collapsed after the disappearance of its founder.

3. Operations

The major operation associated with HS is the murder of `Umar Ben-Jallun (Omar Benjelloun) on Dec. 18, 1975. Ben-Jallun had been a leader of the socialist party USFP (Union Socialiste des Forces Populaires), and the editor of its journal *al-Muharrir*.[7] Details of the murder are murky; it appears that the victim had his head crushed by a sharp heavy object.[8] However, it is by no means absolutely certain that the murder was the responsibility of HS or ordered by Muti`. According to the court Ben-Jallun's assassins consisted of the following group:

1. Ahmad Sa`d
2. Muhammad Mustaqim
3. `Umar Halim
4. Hasan Jabir
5. `Umar Uzukala
6. Hasan Kindi
7. Ahmad Shu`ay
8. `Abd al-`Aziz al-Nu`mani

Al-Nu`mani was apparently the actual killer, and was sentenced to life imprisonment *in absentia*. This cell gives us a sense of what the other cells in the *jihad* section must have looked like. All members of the group that assassinated Ben-Jallun were students. Significantly, al-Nu`mani and his group called themselves Harakat al-Mujahidin al-Maghariba (The Movement of Moroccan Fighters), and eventually formally left HS in 1980,[9] whereupon Muti` founded another *jihad* section called Fasil al-Jihad. With this new group Muti` called for open military operations inside Morocco. However, by 1985 all of its members had been arrested: 71 were tried (20 *in absentia*) in 1983, another group of 26 (nine *in absentia*) were tried in 1985 after a discovery of arms caches.

HS had already been banned prior to the assassination of Ben-Jallun, after it had begun to attract the negative attention of the government. However, the Moroccan

---

went to Spain); Park and Boum, *Dictionary*, p. 186; John Entelis, "Political Islam in the Maghreb," in Entelis (ed), *Islam, Democracy and the State in North Africa* (Bloomington, IN: Indiana University Press, 1997), p. 53.
[7] Interestingly, Muti` himself had once been a member of the USFP; Emad Eldin Shahin, *Political Ascent: Contemporary Islamic Movements in North Africa* (Boulder, CO: Westview Press, 1997), p. 186 details the friendly terms between Benjallun and Muti`.
[8] The conflicting accounts and evidence against the accused is given in *al-Mu'amara*, pp. 29-36, 81-102, including methods of torture used to extract confessions.
[9] *Mu'amara*, p. 28.

authorities accused HS of participating in the January 1984 riots and inciting people to violence. During the following year a number of arms caches were discovered along the Algerian border and further members of the group arrested. It is not clear whether there was indeed a link between the caches and HS, and this discovery might have been simply used as an excuse to round up Muslim extremists.

Muti` by this period had long been in exile from Morocco, and according to some interesting reports had actually participated in the Nov. 1979 attack on the Haram al-Sharif in Mecca by radical Muslims under the leadership of Juhayman al-`Utaybi.[10] Although this attack failed to ignite the messianic response that al-`Utaybi had hoped for, if it is true that Muti` indeed participated, then this would clarify the importance of the group to the larger radical Muslim community.

4. Thought and Influence

Most of Muti`'s thought appears to have been inspired by Marxism, the writings of the Muslim Brotherhood leader and ideologue Hasan al-Banna (d. 1949) and the radical Muslim leader Sayyid Qutb (d. 1966). Muti`'s principle work,[11] *al-Thawrah al-Islamiyya qadar al-Maghrib al-rahin* (*The Islamic Revolution is the Destiny of Present-day Morocco*) is a political-religious call for an Islamic revolution in Morocco, and it is easy to see the reasons why it was controversial in its time (although rather tame today). *Thawrah* begins with a lengthy discussion of the political landscape of Morocco, in which most attention is paid to the leftist parties, and its economic inequalities. It is fairly obvious that Muti` is trying for a more populist note as he discusses the poverty of the masses, and his Marxist roots are clear from the manner in which he describes class warfare.

Muti`'s analysis reveals that he would like to form an Islamic party that will appeal to the masses. He complains that the Marxists have been successful in painting Islam as the value-system of the wealthy and privileged, and he notes that a large number of the wealthy take refuge in an excess of hypocritically pious actions in order to cover up their ill-gotten riches.[12] The monarchy is not spared; he critiques the excessive servility that people, especially the elite closest to the monarchy, demonstrate towards the king, and says that this is not Islamic.

A great deal of *al-Thawra* deals with the issue of foreign domination of Morocco. Muti` discusses the economic power of the Europeans and the French in particular, and

---

[10] Henry Munson, *Religion and Power in Morocco*, p. 161 (citing Burgat, *L'Islamisme au Maghreb*, trans. into English as *The Islamic Movement in North Africa*, p. 150).

[11] I was unable to gain access to his other works, *Malkiyyat al-ard fi al-Islam* (*Ownership of land in Islam*), `Arab wa-Barbar: mu'amara li-tansir al-Maghrib wa-ihtilaliha (`Arabs and Berbers: A Conspiracy to Christianize Morocco and Occupy it*), *Hadd al-saraqa wa-ma`rakat al-`awda ila hakimiyyat al-Islam* (*The Punishment of Theft and the Battle to Return to Islamic Rule*), *al-Tanzim silahan.. bayna al-mathal wa-l-tatbiq* (*Armed Organization.. Between Myth and Reality*), and *Nizam al-hukm al-Islami bayna al-asala wa-l-turathiyya wa-l-taghrib* (*The Islamic Order of Ruling: Between the Origin, the Traditional and the Westernization*). Their contents seem fairly clear from the titles.

[12] Muti`, *al-Thawra al-Islamiyya fi al-Maghrib al-rahin* (Holland (?): al-Shabiba al-Islamiyya, 1984), p. 18.

comes to the conclusion that Morocco is still basically occupied and a colony. He also discusses the issue of the American bases in Morocco, and says that their purpose is to prop up the monarchy and to instill fear in the people. All of these measures have the basic goal of Christianizing Morocco or at least de-Islamizing it. He also denounces the close ties that Morocco has with a number of other pro-western Arab countries, and the Camp David peace agreement between Egypt and Israel in particular. All of these denunciations are political in nature, and Muti` does not once cite a Qur'anic verse or a *hadith* to back up his critique.

Like `Abd al-Salam Faraj's *al-Farida al-gha'iba* (*The Missing Obligation*) Muti`'s *Thawra* emphasizes *jihad* as one of the principal answers to the problems of the Muslims. In order to shore up the legitimacy of *jihad* he cites a variety of historical sources concerning the war of `Abd al-Qadir against the French in Algeria (1832-49) and `Abd al-Karim in the Rif (1920s) and how both had used Islamic slogans and had fought for Islam to humiliate the unbelievers.[13] On page 53 (of 70) he cites the Qur'an for the very first time and proceeds to discuss *hijra* (emigration) and *jihad*.

Muti`'s emphasis is heavily upon the necessity of *hijra* prior to actually fighting *jihad* against the Moroccan government.[14] Presumably he was writing of his own exile from Morocco, and called for his followers to join him. In the end, although he issues ringing calls for the assembly of the armies of God to fight the infidel government, he gives his readers no answers as to how the government is to be fought, and simply says that those who are true in faith will either leave the unbelieving society or wage *jihad* inside of it.

> "Muti`'s emphasis is heavily upon the necessity of *hijra* prior to actually fighting *jihad* against the Moroccan government."

After reading through his pamphlet and others published by the group, it is easy to see why Muti`'s group faltered. Compared to material that was to appear shortly from Egyptian radicals or global jihadists such as `Abd Allah `Azzam (in Pakistan), Muti`'s writings are unsatisfying. His prose is of an elevated style and his analysis is that of a middle-range political commentator, but he does not succeed in making the material, especially the Qur'an and the traditional *jihad* literature, relevant to the situation of Morocco. It is unclear even to what extent he has command of the traditional sources, since he cites them so infrequently. In addition to these flaws, although the manner in which he highlights the problems of Morocco might be correct, he offers no real solutions that would create a modest let alone a mass movement. Probably his only stroke of genius is to attempt to base the Islamic movement squarely upon the large numbers of underprivileged. But even in this attempt he does not approach the problem with proper consideration: most of these masses are in fact already loyal to either Sufi groups (to which he, like all radical Muslims, was hostile) or Marxist groups. Muti` does not offer a reason why HS should or could command their loyalty.

---

[13] Ibid, pp. 49-52.
[14] Ibid, pp. 53-7.

10

5. Conclusions

It is interesting to speculate as to the reasons why al-Suri chose HS over all the other *jihadi* or militant groups that have operated in or from Morocco. One cannot say that his choice of the group was motivated by their success or their prominence, since they achieved neither. In a later section of *al-Da`wa,* al-Suri discusses Moroccans again,[15] and there as well he is curiously imprecise and lacks any specific knowledge. The most obvious conclusion to be reached from this problematic material is that al-Suri simply lacked information but wanted to give as global a presentation of Islamic *jihad* as possible to his reader. Therefore, he had to include something from Morocco, but it may be that he had never been involved enough with fighters from North Africa to know anything about them. This is odd, nonetheless, because his knowledge of Algeria and the anti-governmental *jihad* there is quite deep.

On a slightly different note, there is the additional question of why he chose HS out of all the radical groups that operated in Morocco. HS was far from being popular and probably never had more than several hundred members. Others such as `Abd al-Salam Yassin (founder of a number of radical groups through the 1970s and 1980s) were far more popular and at their peak actually constituted serious threats to the monarchy and could not be ignored. However, HS was, despite its tiny numbers, a genuinely (albeit early) globalist movement. Its radical rejection of the monarchy and especially of King Hasan's annexation of the Western Sahara in 1975 (which gained the monarch popularity that previously he had not enjoyed) had all the hallmarks of a globalist movement. And although HS was aborted at an early phase of its existence, it was organized as a radical Islamic counter-society, somewhat akin to the Jama`a Islamiyya in Indonesia.[16]

---

[15] Al-Suri, *Da`wa*, pp. 612-14.
[16] Which significantly was also revealed prematurely by the commencement of terrorist activities in Bali in 2002.

THE *HARAKAT AL-DAWLA AL-ISLAMIYYA*[17] IN ALGERIA (1973-76 = 1982 - 1987)

1. Historical Background

Al-Suri's presentation of the revolt of Mustafa Bu-`Ali,[18] like that of `Abd al-Karim Muti`'s Haraka al-Shabiba (HS), is problematic and reveals that he most probably did not know the history of the group very well (the true dates of the group are 1982-87). Algeria's history as a locus for Muslim revolt and later for radical Muslim revolt is well-established. From the initial resistance to French conquest marshaled by the great `Abd al-Qadir (1832-47) to the numerous revolts that took place throughout the 19th century against the French colonists,[19] Algeria became a by-word in the Muslim world for fighting. Although the French army succeeded in reducing each one of these groups in its turn, and by the middle of the 20th century had established a powerful settler colony in Algeria, the country was never really pacified.

Starting with an initial revolt in 1945 against the French colonists, the Algerian war of independence was fought with extensive brutalities on both sides between 1954-62.[20] Although this war was not won on the basis of political Islam one cannot deny that there were significant strands of prominent Muslim figures who participated in it. However, the chief fruits of independence went to the leftists who dominated the ruling FLN that took power in 1962 and has held it ever since. Under the rule of Houari Boumedienne (1965-78) the FLN turned strongly to the left and embraced a type of third-worldism (whatever that was supposed to mean) that relegated Islam to a minor role in society.[21] This policy was continued with some modifications leading to a more market economy by Boumedienne's successor, Chadli Bendjedid (1977-1992).

However, the vast majority of Algerians were left out of the prosperity of their country and the liberalization of the 1980s had little effect upon them. There was particular resentment concerning the wealth derived from Algeria's vast oil reserves which was usually confined to a small elite. This elite cultivated the continuation of a French language domination of Algeria so that those who did not know French or did not speak it well had little chance to advance in society.

Algerian society prior to the civil war of 1992-2005 (approximately) was divided into several regions that had little interaction: the region of Algiers and its immediate environs, the Arabic speaking mountainous region close to Algiers, the Berber speaking mountainous region to the east (the Kabyle), the people of the plains beyond the mountains (mostly small villagers), and lastly the desert dwellers to the south. The people of the first two regions were those that had participated in the fighting against the French in the 1954-62 war of independence. That privileged group of fighters constituted the core of the FLN support. But by the 1980s the vast majority of the

---

[17] In al-Suri's text this title seems to be miswritten as Harakat al-Duwaliyya al-Islamiyya, which makes no sense, so it has been corrected to the name written in other sources.
[18] The French spelling of his name is Moustapha Bouali or Bouyali.
[19] Peter von Sivers, "The Realm of Justice: Apocalyptic Revolts in Algeria 1849-1879," *Humaniora Islamica* 1 (1973), pp. 47-60.
[20] For history see Alistair Horne, *A Savage War of Peace: Algeria 1954-62* (London: Papermac, 1996); and Abder Rahmane Derredji, *The Algerian Guerilla Campaign: Strategy and Tactics* (Lewiston, NY: Edwin Mellen Press, 1997).
[21] See Hugh Roberts, *The Battlefield: Algeria 1988-2002*, chapter 13 "Third World, last rites."

population was not part of that privileged group. Some like Abbasi Madani, the founder of the Islamic group Front Islamique du Salut (FIS) were tending more towards an Islamic solution to Algeria's problems.

2. The Harakat al-Dawla al-Islamiyya

Demand for an Islamic state was the core of Mustafa Bu-`Ali's group Harakat al-Dawla al-Islamiyya (The Movement for an Islamic State, HDI). Bu-`Ali himself was one of the original fighters of the FLN who had grown disenchanted with its policies. Within the context of Algeria, political and religious legitimacy, even during the 1980s, was conferred largely upon those who had fought in the War of Independence. Ideologically, Bu-`Ali and his group started their campaign claiming that the Algerian elite was guilty of apostasy similar to the GIA that followed him and must be fought with *jihad*. In this, he followed the tradition of other radical Muslims such as al-Shaykh Mahfuz Nahnah and Muhammad Bu-Sulyamani (who revolted in 1977 and 1980 respectively).[22] But Bu-`Ali and his group were much larger than these two previous violent manifestations and constituted a harbinger of what was to happen in Algeria in the 1990s. However, it is also apparent that Bu-`Ali did not make global accusations of apostasy and focused most of the attention of his group upon symbols of excess in Algeria.

From an organizational point of view, HDI does not seem to have been anything other than a small group based in the mosques of the al-Achour and Notre Dame d'Afrique quarters of Algiers.[23] All of its members apparently fought and preached, and there was no separate organization for preaching and recruitment (*da`wa*) as with the Moroccan Harakat al-Shabiba (HS). Bu-`Ali began his preaching in 1979, and concentrated his activities in the region of Algiers and its closely surrounding suburbs and provinces (e.g., Blida).[24] It seems that Bu-`Ali sought religious legitimacy from the `ulama, including Nahnah, but the latter counseled him not to take the path of violence.[25] Tawil says that the prominent and respected cleric Ahmad Sahnun even had Bu-`Ali ejected from his house to demonstrate that he did not accept his ideas.[26]

However, the younger clerics were much more sympathetic to Bu-`Ali, and looked up to him as a veteran of the 1954-62 war and as a man who was not afraid to speak the truth.[27] Shaykh Rabih Kabir, one of these younger activists, was quoted saying:

> The level of corruption was well known in it [the government]...this is
> what drove him in his conviction that those [the elite] would never be

---

[22] Kumayl al-Tawil, *al-Haraka al-Islamiyya al-musallaha fi al-Jaza'ir* (Beirut: al-Nahar, 1998), p. 55.

[23] Zahra Ben-`Arus, *al-Islamawiyya al-siyasiyya: al-Ma'sat al-Jaza'iriyya* (Beirut: Dar al-Farabi, 2002), p. 64 has accounts of this early period of *da`wa*.

[24] Ibid, p. 55.

[25] Michael Willis, *The Islamist Challenge in Algeria* (Berkshire: Ithaca Press, 1996), cites Ahmed Merah (Bu-`Ali's second-in-command) to say that Nahnah actively informed on Bu-`Ali; see also Ben-`Arus, *Islamawiyya*, pp. 65-6.

[26] Ibid, p. 55; also Willis, *Islamist Challenge in Algeria*, p. 80.

[27] He also had a secret *fatwa* from the respected Shaykh Larbaoui according to Miloud Zaater, *L'Algérie de la guerre á la guerre* (Paris: L'Haramattan, 2003), p. 81.

13

persuaded by anything other than force. But this was the idea of a very small group, even though the people continued to hold Bu-`Ali in esteem and honor, despite the fact that he was a man outside the law fighting against the establishment. The connection between the government and the people had been broken. They saw in the revolt of Bu-`Ali in the mountains and his revolution the realization of their dream [of an Islamic state?].[28]

However, Rabih, whose group was based in Constantine, said that while he and his supporters referred to Bu-`Ali as a fighter (*mujahid*), they did not render him any active aid.

Francois Burgat cites Bu-`Ali's brother-in-law (at the time an imam in Marseilles) to say that the latter only went underground because the authorities had killed Bu-`Ali's brother and raped his sister-in-law.[29] At the end of his "run",[30] Bu-`Ali was killed by security personnel on Jan. 3, 1987 together with three of his followers.[31] There are a great many questions about how this was accomplished. According to one account, Bu-`Ali's driver was taken and tortured by the authorities, who released him and allowed him to resume his function as driver in return for intelligence concerning the movements of Bu-`Ali. The driver is said to have been killed in the attack on Bu-`Ali's vehicle.[32] The trial of MIA (Mouvement Islamiste Algérien) followers of Bu-`Ali took place in July 1987 with 202 defendants only 15 of whom were sentenced to death.[33] Mansur Milyani, `Abd al-Qadir Chebouti and Muhammad La`mamara, the three senior lieutenants of Bu-`Ali were all sentenced to death. However, Bendjedid pardoned the followers of Bu-`Ali in March 1989, and allowed them to re-enter society.[34] This they did until the beginning of the civil war in 1991-2 when all three took up arms again.

3. Prominent Operations and Personnel

Most of HDI's operations were carried out by the group that was founded by Bu-`Ali as its armed wing, the Mouvement Islamiste Algérien in 1982. The MIA was to last much longer than HDI and have a deeper influence over the course of events during the Algerian civil war. Its operations are usually considered to have taken place between 1981-87:

1. April 1981, an attack in Oran (with planned attacks upon the Aurassi Hotel in central Algiers and the airport that were aborted);

---

[28] Ibid, p.56.
[29] Francois Burgat, *The Islamic Movement in North Africa*. Trans. William Dowell (Austin: University of Texas Press, 1997), p. 116.
[30] Using the term of Hugh Roberts, *Battlefield*, p. 23.
[31] Tawil, p. 56; Riccardo Rene Laremont, *Islam and the Politics of Resistance in Algeria* (Trenton, N.J.: Africa World Press, 2001), p. 190; but Martinez, *Algerian Civil War*, p. 49 note 4 (citing Burgat) says Feb. 3; while Martin Stone, *The Agony of Algeria* (New York: Columbia University Press, 1997), p. 182 says March 1.
[32] Tawil, p. 87 note 7.
[33] Willis, *Islamist Challenge*, p. 82.
[34] John Entelis, "Political Islam in the Maghreb," in Entelis (ed), *Islam, Democracy and the State in North Africa* (Bloomington: Indiana University Press, 1997), p. 62.

2. July 1981 a planned attack on the headquarters of the Union Nationale des Femmes Algériennes in Algiers;
3. August 1985 a highjack of a payroll from a factory near Algiers and an attack on a police school at Souma (resulting in the death of a cadet and the seizure of arms);
4. 1985: removal to the mountains at Larba under pressure by the army;[35] and
5. Death of Mustafa Bu-`Ali Jan. 3, 1987.

Bu-`Ali and his group were frequently accused of attempting to assassinate prominent members of the regime but none of these assassinations were ever successful and the evidence concerning them is slender.[36] Burgat lists the planned assassination of a prime minister (Bendjedid) on Dec. 9, 1982, the possible assassination of the deputy leader of the FLN, a possible kidnapping of a western ambassador and bombings of war monuments that were resented by the radical Muslims in Algiers (because they were statues).[37]

It seems that Bu-`Ali chose his targets specifically because of their connections with the corruption of the state which was the basis for his revolt. Hence, attacks against a prominent mall or the airport made perfect sense. The planned attack on the organization of Algerian women was also a harbinger of the attacks that radical Muslims would make upon prominent feminists in the 1990s and early 2000s. All of these are symbolic

> "Bu-`Ali was very careful not to target civilians and to butcher them in the name of *takfir* as the GIA was doing."

attacks upon the non-Islamic elements in Algerian society. But, as Burgat pointed out, HDI and the Bu-`Ali incarnation of MIA consistently sought to avoid random killings of civilians, and those non-combatants who were killed were killed accidentally. Again, this methodology is in sharp contrast to the developing attitudes of radical Muslims in Egypt, who had already rationalized the indiscriminant killing of Muslims, and to the later GIA.

Very little is known about Bu-`Ali's methods of fighting. He apparently chose the region of Larba, located almost directly south of the capital Algiers, at the gateway to the mountains that separate northern Algeria from the plains and the Sahara Desert, because it was his home. This location was strategic in many ways, however; the government simply could not afford to let a rebel control this area as the road going through Larba was a major artery leading to the oil rich south. But by the same token, it was very easy for Bu-`Ali to find allies in this region, and because of the mountainous terrain and the fact that he had fought in this region before against the French, it was easy for him to defend himself. Hence his ability to survive against the government forces for almost two full years on the run (1985-7).

---

[35] List taken from Stone, *Agony*, pp. 181-2; see also Willis, *Challenge*, pp. 81-2; Ben-`Arus, *Islamawiyya*, pp. 66-7.
[36] Tawil, p. 56.
[37] Burgat, *Islamic Movement*, pp. 112, 266.

4. Influence

After the death of Bu-`Ali the leadership of MIA (by this time probably more an acronym for Mouvement Islamique Armeé) passed to `Abd al-Qadir Chebouti, who continued to lead it well into the period of the Algerian civil war.[38] However, the problems of the group continued. After the disastrous cancellation of the 1991 elections by the army—as a result of the overwhelming victory of the FIS—there was a great deal of anger throughout sections of Algeria. This anger was focused on those regions that had supported or tolerated the HDI and the MIA, and consequently a great many young men wanted to join the violent group in order to take vengeance upon the government. Ironically, while Bu-`Ali had been alive and sought to found an Islamic state, the founder of FIS, Abbasi Madani, had opposed his activist campaign, and had actively confronted the HDI in mosques where he had preached during the early 1980s.[39]

It is very possible that the system of farming out franchises of *jihad* throughout the suburbs of Algiers and the neighboring larger cities was the result of Bu-`Ali's methods. Martinez, in his *The Algerian Civil War*, describes how each neighborhood during the period 1992-4 had its own *amir*, usually associated with the GIA, but sometimes with other groups as well, or unaffiliated. However, this method, while allowing the maximum possible individual freedom to these "entrepreneurs" also made fighting the war against the authorities overall extremely difficult and encouraged the rise of local warlords and bullies who alienated the population. Martinez also details how this "entrepreneurial" policy was also to the benefit of the security forces since the latter knew that they could just let these neighborhood *amir*s wither away as they became more and more unpopular.[40]

Unfortunately for the MIA, one of the lessons that it had learned as a result of the betrayal of Bu-`Ali in 1987 was that in order to be successful one had to be cautious about admitting new members, and consequently the MIA was ill-prepared for the inundation of possible recruits in the spring of 1992.[41] This attitude of caution was warranted in a small guerilla group that had to protect itself, but was not suited for a mass movement. For this reason the MIA failed to accept the wave of potential recruits who had no choice but to go to other organizations, or even founded them by themselves.

Chebouti himself continued to play an important role in the Algerian civil war. Although the MIA was never the dominant faction in the early stages of the fighting, eventually by July 1994—under some pressure due to the success of the GIA at that time—Chebouti arranged to gather a number of *mujahidin* groups together under his leadership. This new organization was called Armé Islamiques du Salut (AIS) and later proclaimed its allegiance to the FIS.[42] The MIA and the AIS that succeeded it fought very much in the tradition of the *maquis* of 1954-62 and disassociated themselves with

---

[38] Azzedine Layachi, "Political Liberalisation and the Islamist Movement in Algeria," in Michael Bonner, Megan Reif and Mark Tessler (eds), *Islam, Democracy and the State in Algeria: Lessons for the Western Mediterranean and Beyond* (New York: Routledge, 2005), pp. 50-1.
[39] Willis, *Challenge*, p. 80.
[40] Full discussion in Martinez, *Algerian Civil War*, chapters 4-5.
[41] Martinez, *Algerian Civil War*, pp. 68-71.
[42] Willis, *Islamist Challenge*, pp. 327-8.

the blanket attacks upon civilians that the GIA claimed. Instead they concentrated their attention upon military and police targets. However, Chebouti himself no longer wielded absolute power because of his poor health and younger leadership quickly came to the fore.

Mansur Milyani took a different route, and after he separated himself from Chebouti, he went on to found the GIA. However, he also never achieved any domination within the GIA and his leadership role was seen as part of the effort of the new group to gain legitimacy by embracing some of the old MIA leaders.[43]

5. Conclusions

Bu-`Ali appears to have been a simple, pious man who saw himself thrust into a role rather than seeking it out. As previously stated, he did not leave any known writings, and appeared to present himself as being a man who was willing to preach and fight for an Islamic state when others were not. Burgat cites him to say that he was willing to stand aside if someone more suitable would take over the job.[44] Although this might have been false modesty, there is little in the historical record that indicates him to have been anything other than a plain-spoken fighter. He apparently sought to recreate the atmosphere of the resistance to the French within the mountain villages and towns of Algeria, and eventually perhaps create a mass revolution. His tragedy was that he was simply not competent to carry out such a plan. It is also clear from reading the statements ascribed to him that he knew little of contemporary radical Muslim thought and apparently was not intellectually dependent upon non-Algerians. He was a nationalist radical Muslim rather than a globalist.[45]

> "[Bu- `Ali] knew little of contemporary radical Muslim thought... He was a nationalist radical Muslim rather than a globalist.

The HDI and the MIA of Mustafa Bu-`Ali are listed in al-Suri's book as precursors of the GIA and al-Jama`a al-Salafiyya li'l-Da`wa wa-l-Qital (GSPC).[46] The ideology of both groups was based upon a militant confrontation with the secular government of Algeria. In this regard they stood in opposition to most of the other Islamic radicals of their time, including the FIS which had closer relations (both personally and ideologically) with the ruling FLN.[47] However, Bu-`Ali was not a writer and, unlike the prolific leaders of the FIS (and other Islamic groups), he apparently never penned a political manifesto. Apparently it is due to this fact that al-Suri, like with the Harakat al-Shabiba of Morocco, made so many mistakes concerning the group.

Abu Hamza al-Misri in his *Khawarij and Jihad*, written in order to disassociate the radical Muslim community in the U.K. from the massacres perpetrated by the GIA during the period 1994-98, highlights another point. He says that Bu-`Ali was very

---

[43] Tawil, pp. 145-54.
[44] Burgat, *Islamic Movement*, p. 262.
[45] Ben-`Arus, *Islamawiyya*, p. 68.
[46] They were also seen in this light by the British radical Abu Hamza al-Misri, *Khawaarij and Jihad* (Birmingham: Maktabat al-Ansar, n.d.), p. 145.
[47] Roberts, *Battlefield*, chapter 4, esp. p. 95.

careful not to target civilians and to butcher them in the name of *takfir* as the GIA was doing. While this analysis might be too generous—since Bu-`Ali and his group did plan such attacks—it may be that al-Suri highlights HDI and MIA precisely because of that fact. Al-Suri was well aware, as is revealed in his analysis of the experience of the Algerian radicals of the 1990s[48] that one of the principal reasons for the failure of the Algerian *jihad* was in fact the global *takfir* that was leveled against the entirety of Algerian society and the massacres of innocents that followed in its wake. This critical mistake enabled the Algerian authorities to portray the radicals as barbaric and eventually caused them to lose support and split. The GSPC, successor to the GIA in 1998, in its founding covenant, says that it will not participate in global *takfir* or slaughter in an indiscriminant manner.[49]

---

[48] Al-Suri, *Da`wa*, pp. 604-6.
[49] See *Mithaq al-Jama`a al-Salafiyya li'l-Da`wa wa-l-Qital*, pp. 8f. 12-14, etc.

THE AFGHANI ARABS IN LEBANON UNDER ABU `A'ISHA AL-LUBNANI

1. Lebanon: History of Conflict and Civil War

Lebanon is part of the Levant, the heart of greater Syria, and the prime location for minorities and outsiders in the Middle East to take refuge. This history of being a refuge is due to Lebanon's geography, which is divided into four distinct regions. The coastal region, containing the great port cities of Beirut, Tyre, Sidon and Tripoli, is home to most of the population. It is a fertile region that is well-watered by rains from the Mediterranean Sea and endowed with lush vegetation, but is still mild in climate. However, the second region, that of the Lebanon Mountains, rises steeply behind it. These mountains continue into northern Israel, and leaving Lebanon to the north they rise in altitude along coastal Syria. Further inland there is the great plain of the Baqa`a Valley, lush and green, well-watered from mountainous run-off and the top-soil that comes with it. Then lastly, the Anti-Lebanon Mountains rise even higher than the Lebanon Mountains dividing Lebanon from the capital of Syria, Damascus.

The human geography of Lebanon is divided by religion. Because the country is such a natural destination for religious minorities, Lebanon does not have one majority, but a series of almost equally divided minorities. In the broadest sense, the division is between Muslims (approximately 50% of the population), Christians (approximately 40%) and Druze (approximately 10%) with other scattered minority groups. However, this division does not accurately reflect the internal divisions of the larger religious groups, especially those of Islam and Christianity.

Muslims are divided into Sunnis, who are located in the western section of Beirut and around the northern region of Tripoli. Shi`ites are located in the vast southern slums of Beirut (called the "belt of misery") and throughout southern Lebanon and in the Baqa`a Valley up to Ba`albek. Christians are equally divided into the long-dominant Maronite Catholics, the Greek Orthodox and the Armenians, with other smaller denominations scattered throughout. Maronite Christians are located around eastern Beirut and the mountains behind it, and along the coast up to the region of Tripoli, and some in the south. Greek Orthodox predominate near the Muslim areas of Beirut, and in the Baqa`a town of Zahle. Druze are located in their home of the Shuf Mountains. Despite the long civil war, a great deal of overlapping occurs—except that the division between Muslim and Christian Beirut is still crystal clear (even nearly 15 years after the end of the civil war).

Recent Lebanese history was dominated by the civil war. Prior to 1975, the country was dominated by the Maronites together with the Sunni elite of Beirut and Tripoli. But due to population changes, the Maronites and Sunnis gradually began to weaken in favor of the Shi`ites of the south. The civil war, however, was sparked to a large extent by the influx of large numbers of Palestinians—who were Sunni, but not part of the Sunni elite—that were placed in what were intended to have been short-term refugee camps mostly in the south. Gradually throughout the 1970s the Palestinians built up a mini-state in the south that was terminated by the Israeli invasion of 1982-5. This latter invasion had been designed to both bring the Palestinian mini-state to an end as well as to shore up the Christian Maronite domination of Lebanon, then severely weakened by the reverses Christians had suffered during the previous 10

19

years. However, in actuality the Israeli invasion paved the way for a Shi`ite revival and eventual domination over southern Lebanon that was completed after Israel's withdrawal in 2000.

"Al-Suri, in his discussion of Abu `A'isha, admits that he knew very few Lebanese who fought in Afghanistan"

The Lebanese civil war came to an end in 1990 with the Ta'if Agreements in which the various Lebanese religious groups agreed to reapportion power in a more equitable manner. This agreement strengthened the role of Syria, which had effectively occupied a large chunk of the northern region of the country since 1976, in keeping peace between the different groups. It also mandated the much greater power role given to Shi`ites, and effectively confined the Palestinians to their camps and ignored them. The Palestinian refugees were also sidelined by another regional development at that time, the Oslo accords between the Palestinian Liberation Organization and Israel in 1993. While originally the Palestinian refugees in Lebanon had expected to be repatriated to their original homes in Israel under any peace agreement, effectively the PLO had agreed to ignore the refugees in Lebanon and to make an agreement on the basis of a state in the West Bank and the Gaza strip. This agreement did not touch upon the aspirations of the Palestinian refugees in Lebanon or answer the question of what should be done with them. It was fairly natural, then, given this state of limbo, that the refugees in southern Lebanon—cut out of both of the major political processes of the early 1990s—would turn to radical Islam as a panacea.

2. The Experience of the Afghani Arabs

Abu `A'isha al-Lubnani, the *nom de guerre* of Bassam Kanj, was brought together with the other members of the Lebanese radical Islamic group by his experience in Afghanistan and then later in the United States. After the invasion of Afghanistan by the U.S.S.R., numbers of Muslims worldwide came to Peshawar, Pakistan, responding to the call of the charismatic Palestinian radical *jihad* leader `Abd Allah `Azzam (assassinated 1989). Most of these were Arabs, and many of those were either from Saudi Arabia, Yemen or North Africa. Al-Suri, in his discussion of Abu `A'isha, admits that he knew very few Lebanese who fought in Afghanistan,[50] and it is very likely that their numbers did not reach more than 200. Indeed, it is difficult to imagine that when Lebanon was itself a battlefield that very many Lebanese would have wanted to go to Afghanistan.

But as the Lebanese war was winding down in 1990, Bassam Kanj went to Afghanistan, and trained in the Khalden camp, where he stayed for the next 4-5 years. It was in Afghanistan that he met with Raed Hijazi, Nabil al-Marabh and Muhammad Kamal al-Zahabi, all of whom would be linked to various different radical Muslim or al-Qa`ida plots during the late 1990s up until Sept. 11, 2001. It is difficult to assess the nature of the training that they underwent, and hard to believe that they actually saw much fighting. For the most part the experience of the Afghani Arabs—as they were called during the 1990s—was not so much a military one as a psychological and a religious

---

[50] Al-Suri, *Da`wa*, p. 614.

epiphany. It was in Afghanistan that they were finally given the opportunity to join together with Muslims from all over the world and oppose a common enemy.

Although the Afghani factions failed to unite in the immediate aftermath of the Soviet withdrawal (1989) and it was not until 1992 that they were able to conquer Kabul, the capital, the Afghani Arabs enjoyed a tremendous burst of confidence as a result of their role (apparently) in the defeat of the U.S.S.R. and its subsequent collapse. This confidence was married to the fact that they were effectively stateless—since most of their home states did not want them back—and bound together by ties of battle and their common Islamic faith. For this reason when they did go back to their home countries, such as Algeria or Egypt, it was mainly to found anti-governmental *jihad* groups, or to move on to other battlefields such as Bosnia-Herzegovina or Chechnya. Some went and immersed themselves into European or American life as well.

3. The American Connection

The Lebanese al-Qaʿida group of Abu ʿAʾisha is interesting in that it was composed of people with close connections to the United States or who had lived in fact there for a number of years. Abu ʿAʾisha himself was Palestinian, apparently from Lebanon, who came to Boston to work as a taxi driver with the Boston Cab Company. Raed Hijazi was also of Palestinian origin, but had been born in California and was apparently Americanized. By 1998 he was working for the Boston Cab Company as well. He had gone to Afghanistan approximately in 1990 and stayed for four years. Nabil al-Marabh, a Palestinian born in Kuwait, had returned to Canada where he had previously lived in Feb. 1994, and had come to the U.S. in June 1995 (where his application for asylum was denied). Muhammad al-Zahabi moved from New York to Boston in 1997 and took a job with the same company.[51] This group was apparently an al-Qaʿida sleeper cell that was in communication with top al-Qaʿida operatives such as Abu Zubayda and Khalid Shaykh Muhammad.

In retrospect it seems clear that there was a group of related plots that were to come to fruition either because of this group or with their aid. One of these plots was that of Raed Hijazi, who had taken the *nom de guerre* of Abu Ahmad the American, and was supposed to coordinate a series of terror attacks in Jordan at the end of 1999. These included the bombing of the Radisson Hotel,[52] the tourist sites of Mt. Nebo (traditional site of the death of Moses), Christian churches in Jordan and possibly the Queen Alia Airport in Amman.[53] Since these attacks were supposed to be coordinated with the attack on the Los Angles airport to be carried out by Ahmad Ressam (arrested Dec. 14, 1999) at the end of 1999, they were dubbed the "Millennium Plot."[54] Hijazi had passed through Jordan, but had gone on to Syria and so was absent when the

---

[51] See cooperativeresearch.org "Profile: Raed Hijazi"; "Profile: Bassam Kanj"; "Context of Early 1997-Late 1998."
[52] Although Hijazi's attack was not successful, six years later almost to the day (Nov. 8, 2005) the al-Qaʿida in Iraq faction of Abu Musaʿb al-Zarqawi would carry out suicide attacks there killing nearly 60 people.
[53] See Judith Miller, "Dissecting a Terror Plot from Amman," *New York Times* (Jan. 15, 2001); "Jordanian Court issues Death Sentences in Terror Plot," ict.org (Feb. 12, 2002); and the discussion in *the 9/11 Commission Report* (New York: W.H. Norton, 2004), pp. 175f.
[54] *60 Minutes II:* "The Millennium Plot," at cbsnews.com (Dec. 26, 2001).

Jordanians arrested his group; the Syrians extradited him later and he was condemned to death Feb. 12, 2002.

Hijazi most likely had the easiest time of all the members of this group because as an American-born citizen, he was able to move with considerable freedom around the globe. Both al-Marabh and al-Zahabi had to continually deal with problems due to the fact that they were in the United States illegally (since al-Marabh's request for asylum had been denied) and could not move freely. But al-Marabh still was connected in several ways to the attackers of Sept. 11, 2001 and was arrested for a time until he was deported to Syria in Jan. 2004 since there was no evidence against him.[55] Al-Zahabi seems to have been the least involved in any of the terrorist plots, although he claims to have known Khalid Shaykh Muhammad and Abu Mus`ab al-Zarqawi, and fought in Chechnya between 1999-2000.[56] He was also involved with sending supplies to radical Muslim fighters in Pakistan and was probably more of a facilitator.

Unraveling the tangled web of contacts between the various men reveals that the bonds forged in the camps of Afghanistan were very powerful and held them together for years after the events of the late 1980s and early 1990s. Yet, however grandiose their plans were, they were dwarfed by the ambitions of Abu `A'isha al-Lubnani.

4. Setting up an Islamic State

The most mysterious and poorly documented effort of the ring of four Boston Cab Company drivers was that of Abu `A'isha. Very little is known about the group he founded, which in some of the literature is called al-Dinniyya.[57] In his portrayal of Abu `A'isha, al-Suri lauds the group for fighting against the neo-Sufi group, the Ahbash.[58] The Ahbash, or the Habashis as they are frequently called, are an eclectic group founded by an East African Muslim named `Abdallah b. Muhammad al-Harari al-Shibli al-Abdari (known as al-Habashi, the Ethiopian). For the most part, the teachings of the Ahbash are in diametrical opposition to those of radical Islam, especially global *jihad*. The Ahbash are Sufis, for the most part quietist, avoid calls for a Muslim state or involvement in the political sphere. They have cultivated a close and non-confrontational relationship with Shi`ites and avoid practicing *takfir* (labeling other Muslims unbelievers). All of these elements make them obnoxious to radical Muslims,[59] but within the context of Lebanon, the group is popular among middle class Sunnis and was favored by the Syrian occupation forces (with the claim by their enemies that they were used by the Syrian intelligence network).[60]

---

[55] Stephen Kurkjian and Peter DeMarco, "FBI Probes 'sleeper cell' possibility: Investigation of ex-Boston cabdriver extends to 9/11," *The Boston Globe* at boston.com (June 27, 2004).
[56] Shelley Murphy, "Cab Driver charged with lying to FBI," *The Boston Globe* at boston.com (June 26, 2004).
[57] Named because of the district, al-Dinniyya, where they tried to take power.
[58] Al-Suri, p. 614.
[59] For example, see the refutation of Abu Zakariya, *A Warning and Refutation of the Heretical Group known as Habashis. Translated Excerpts from `Abdallah Muhammad al-Shami's al-Radd `ala `Abdallah al-Habashi* (Warminster, Penn.: AlgebraTan Publishing, 1994).
[60] See the full analysis by A. Nizar Hamzeh and R. Hrair Dekmejian, "A Sufi Response to Political Islamism: al-Ahbash of Lebanon," *International Journal of Middle Eastern Studies* 28 (1996), pp. 217-29.

However, al-Suri seems to claim that the Dinniyya was responsible for the assassination of their Lebanese president Nizar al-Halabi on Aug. 31, 1995, which seems unlikely. This assassination is usually associated with other Sunni radical groups such as Asbat al-Ansar (based in the Palestinian refugee camp of `Ayn al-Hilwa) who did indeed loathe the Ahbash.[61] However, since the Asbat al-Ansar supported the efforts of Abu `A'isha and his close followers to establish a Muslim state in the hills behind Tripoli during the fall of 1999 and gave them refuge after its failure there may be some overlap. Just at the same time as Raed Hijazi was coordinating the millennium plot in Jordan, Abu `A'isha had apparently returned to Lebanon and gone north to Tripoli, which had always been a Sunni stronghold. From there he gathered about 200-300 radicals, among them some Afghani Arabs, and began to take over villages in the region during December 1999-January 2000.

Few of his subordinates' names are known. His lieutenants appear to have been Ahmad Mikati (Abu Bakr), `Ali `Abduh (Abu `Abd al-Rahman) and Sa`d al-Din (frequently sp. Saadeddine) Seiss (Abu Hamza).[62] Other members appear to have included Muhammad Radwan Mahmud (Abu Thabit)[63] and Abu Ramez Sahmarani.[64] There is no other information on the followers, but presumably they were supported by Asbat al-Ansar, who during the course of the fighting, attacked the Russian Embassy in Beirut (Jan. 3, 2000) with a rocket propelled grenade launcher and small arms fire killing a guard.[65] But of the actual fighting there are no reports. Apparently the supporters of Abu `A'isha fought with units of the regular Lebanese Army, and then with the Syrian Army as well. This would not be surprising, as the region of Tripoli is located close to Syria, and Syria enjoyed widespread support from the local population. It is doubtful that the Syrians would have viewed the establishment of an Islamic state there with favor.

It is usually believed that the vast majority of the 200-300 followers of Abu `A'isha died during the course of these battles. His own death is obscure; his widow, an American woman by the name of Marlene al-Mirabi (remarried to a Saudi after his death) mentions that he supposedly fell from a water tower, but that she also saw pictures of him with a bullet hole in the forehead.[66] However, most of the men listed above managed to make their way to the `Ayn al-Hilwa refugee camp where they stayed, immune from capture, for the following years.[67] Their presence in the camp under the protection of the Asbat al-Ansar strengthens the conclusion that this was a joint operation run by the two groups. By 2004 a number of them, including their leader Ahmed Mikati, were in custody under charges of plotting to blow up the Italian Embassy and the Ukrainian consulate in Beirut.[68]

---

[61] It is possible that because al-Suri was writing some five years after the event that the original separation between the Dinniyeh group and the Asbat al-Ansar was not remembered, and for this reason he grouped them together in his presentation.

[62] Gary Gambill, "Ain al-Hilweh: Lebanon's 'Zone of Unlaw'," *Middle East Intelligence Bulletin* 5:6 (June 2003).

[63] "Dinniyeh rebels to disarm," at lebaneseforces.com (Aug. 15, 2002).

[64] Interview in *al-Ahram* (Aug. 15-21, 2002).

[65] www.un.org/documents/ga/docs/55/a55164a2.pdf.

[66] Dan Malone, "Prisoners with Arab Names," at prisonactivist.org (May 9, 2002).

[67] See Gambill, "Ain al-Hilweh," *op. cit.*

[68] Zeina Karam, "35 Accused of Qaeda-linked Plot to bomb targets in Lebanon," *The Boston Globe* at boston.com (Oct. 3, 2004).

5. Conclusions

It is difficult to understand what exactly the Dinniyya group hoped to accomplish. Even working under the assumption that they had a firm alliance with the Asbat al-Ansar it is difficult to understand why they thought—or if they thought—that their operation would be a successful one. The region of Tripoli was in 2000 almost completely controlled by the Syrian Army, and the balance of the Sunnis, while perhaps favorable to certain elements of radical Islam, would certainly not have been sympathetic to a group of outsiders establishing a state in their midst. Nor is it easy to understand what kind of practical aid Asbat al-Ansar could have rendered to the Dinniyya group, as the `Ayn al-Hilwa camp is closely monitored by the Lebanese Army—who know it to be a hotbed of unrest—and in any case is separated from the region of Tripoli by the city of Beirut and the Maronite enclave of Mt. Lebanon.

If one assumes that Kanj and his group were truly influenced by the events in the radical Muslim world around them, perhaps they believed that in the mountainous terrain of northern Lebanon they could establish a base similar to the bases established in Afghanistan and fight a war similar to the one that was then being fought in Chechnya (where al-Zahabi had gone during that same period). But it is still difficult to know who exactly their enemy was, and why Kanj chose this location. Perhaps he realized that his hard-line Sunni group would have no chance establishing itself in the south of Lebanon, controlled then, as now, by Hizb Allah.

The experience of the Lebanese Afghans is the most obscure of all the paradigmatic *jihadi* groups described by al-Suri. Why was it included at all? From the tone of his writing, it seems that al-Suri admired the audacity of this particular operation even if he himself had virtually no information about it (about half of the material that he presents is either unconfirmed or inaccurate). Or perhaps this was his way of including Lebanon within the number of paradigmatic *jihadi* operations he cites; otherwise all of the glory in that country would go to the Shi`ite Hizb Allah.

The (Islamic) Army of Aden Abyan

1. Background of the (Islamic) Army of Aden Abyan

Abu Musa`b al-Suri in his voluminous *Da`wat al-muqawama al-Islamiyya al-`alamiyya* (The Call for Global Islamic Resistance) covers the Islamic Army of Aden Abyan as the ninth of his paradigmatic *jihadi* movements (although it is grouped together with efforts of Bin Laden to start armed Islamic activity in Yemen as well).[69] The origin of the name of the Islamic Army of Aden Abyan (IAAA)[70] is from the well-known apocalyptic tradition in which the Prophet Muhammad is said to have stated: "Twelve thousand will appear from Aden Abyan who will aid God and His Messenger."[71] This tradition usually appears in the context of the wars of the end of the world in which it is said that these

> "Radical Islam has found a fertile field in Yemen."

Muslims from Aden Abyan will be on camel and ride to the aid of the Muslims in Syria. Although it is unclear what Aden Abyan meant in the 8th century, the fact that Abyan is today a province northeast of the present-day city of Aden is sufficient to make the connection radical Muslims want.[72]

Yemen is a torn country located in the southwestern corner of the Arabian Peninsula. Historically it was called Arabia Felix because of its more mountainous, cooler and agriculturally friendly terrain (as opposed to Arabia Petraea, rocky Arabia), and it also receives a substantial rainfall from the seasonal monsoon. However, from a political and religious point of view, it is not highly favored. Historically Yemen was the home of the moderate Zaydi Shi`ite sect, which still constitutes about a quarter of the population in the northern part of the country. Northern Yemen was ruled as an autocracy by a Zaydi Imam (claiming descent from the Prophet Muhammad) until the revolution in 1962. Southern Yemen, the area of Aden, was ruled by the British from India, although effectively the British had little control over the tribal areas surrounding the port of Aden.

In 1967, after a lengthy guerilla campaign, the British were forced out of Aden and the new country drifted into a radical Marxist orbit, becoming the only Arab country to openly attempt to apply Marxism-Leninism. When the Marxist regime of southern Yemen collapsed in 1990, the two countries were united. But in actuality they remained divided. Most of the population of north Yemen was quite conservative and uneducated; south Yemen had a smaller population (only a quarter the size of that of north Yemen), but for all its rejection of Marxism was much more open and well-educated. Women's rights groups had some popularity in the south where many women feared the conservative Islam of the north. The northerners, for their part, treated the south like a colony and swarmed over it, imposing their more conservative

---

[69] *Da`wat al-muqawama al-Islamiyya al-`alamiyya*, pp. 607-8, 610-12.

[70] Since this group goes by a number of different names, not all of which include the term "Islamic" in them, I have placed it in parentheses.

[71] See my *Studies in Muslim Apocalyptic* (Princeton: Darwin Press, 2003), p. 366; and full references in Wensinck (ed.), *Concordance et Indices de la Tradition Musulmane* (Leiden: E.J. Brill, 1936-62), s.v., "`Adan."

[72] The tradition was also validated by the radical Saudi shaykh Sulayman al-`Ulwan in a fatwa in 2003 (*tashih hadith khuruj al-muqatilin min `Adan wa'l-mubashsharat bi-nusrat hadha al-din*), available on tawhed.ws.

norms. These differences led to a civil war in 1994 in which the south was crushed. Ever since, the southerners have been quite discontented and open to any form of protest movement against the northerners.

In general, Yemen is dominated by tribal issues and the miserable economic situation. Effectively, a great deal of the country is only under intermittent government control. Since the country, as an International Crisis Group report said, "is awash with small arms,"[73] there are frequent clashes concerning local issues or honor-based disputes. Many times these are resolved by kidnapping foreigners who are used as negotiating chips by tribesmen. In general, these kidnappings have been resolved without violence; those of the radical Islamists stand out. Economic issues are very problematic for Yemen, which has one of the highest birth rates in the world and cannot support its population. Until 1990-1, many Yemenis worked in neighboring Saudi Arabia and sent money home to their families. However, as a result of widespread support for Saddam Husayn's invasion and occupation of Kuwait that year, these guest-workers were expelled. During the last 15 years, many have gone back to work in Saudi Arabia or other Gulf states, but even so, Yemen has no serious foreign trade other than in coffee.

Radical Islam has found a fertile field in Yemen. There are many radical groups in the country, and their ties to each other are usually unclear—most probably social and educational rather than operational. Al-Qa`ida has had wide support throughout Yemen, where Usama b. Ladin is admired (especially since Yemen, Hadramawt specifically, is his ancestral homeland), and a large number of al-Qa`ida operatives have come from the country. In addition to the Islamic Army of Aden Abyan (IAAA), there is the Shabab al-Mu'minin led by Badr al-Din al-Huthi, which has its basis in the Zaydi (Shi`a) sect of northern Yemen. A group called al-Jihad al-Islami was responsible for the 1992 attack on the U.S. Marines in the Aden Hotel, and IAAA is usually considered to have been a branch of it.[74] Al-Qa`ida itself has a branch in Yemen, which was led by Abu `Ali al-Harithi (assassinated in 2002 by a U.S. missile), and then by `Abd al-Rahim al-Nashiri.[75] All of these groups operate in fairly close quarters, and sometimes cooperate with each other (although there can be hostility between the Sunni pro-al-Qa`ida elements and the Zaydis on doctrinal grounds), and their leaders are usually tied together by educational, social or religious bonds.

2. Personnel and Connections of the Islamic Army of Aden Abyan

Like al-Qa`ida, IAAA got its start in Afghanistan. There were an estimated 27,000 Yemenis that fought in Afghanistan against the Soviet occupation. IAAA's first leader, Abu al-Hasan Zayn al-`Abidin al-Mihdar,[76] was one such fighter. Apparently while he was in Afghanistan he met Abu Hamza al-Misri (Mustafa Kamal), the hook-handed leader of radical Muslims in the U.K., who was to found the group Supporters of

---

[73] ICG report "Yemen: Coping with Terrorism and Violence in a Fragile State," p. 1 (Jan. 8, 2003); al-Suri agrees, and cites almost the same figures (p. 607).

[74] B. Raman, "Attack on the U.S.S. Cole: Background," (Oct. 16, 2000) http://www.ict.org.il/articles/articledet.cfm?articleid=136.

[75] See Arafat Mudabish, "Jihadist Groups in Yemen," *al-Sharq al-Awsat*, April 4, 2006.

[76] There are many ways in which his name and others in this paper are spelled throughout the sources; I am using the standard Arabic transliteration.

Shari`a and become the mouthpiece of the IAAA. Mihdar was leader of IAAA between its founding in either 1996 or 1997 and his arrest at the end of 1998 after the disastrous tourist kidnapping operation. He was executed Oct. 17, 1999 following a trial.

His successor was Khalid `Abd al-Nabi.[77] `Abd al-Nabi, who had fought in Afghanistan like al-Mihdar (he was 37 in 2004). It is unclear how or why `Abd al-Nabi was chosen, and his leadership role does not seem to be very prominent. Presumably he has ties to al-Qa`ida (despite his continual denials), and if IAAA is actually associated with the operations detailed below, then either his control over his supporters is weak or his connections to al-Qa`ida are substantial. He was supposedly killed in clashes with government forces in Oct. 2003 in Abyan province,[78] but then was pardoned by President `Ali `Abd Allah Salih in Nov. 2003, and has since been interviewed several times by the Arab media. Each time he has maintained that IAAA does not exist, a statement that his interviewers regard with skepticism.[79]

IAAA consisted of the following members who can be named and to some extent traced:

> 1. Usama al-Misri (Egyptian), operations leader killed Dec. 1998. This figure is usually said to have been connected to Egyptian Islamic Jihad, but how he came to be part of IAAA is unclear;
> 2. Ahmad Muhammad `Ali `Atif (Yemeni, age 26), acquitted during the trial in 1998;
> 3. Sa`d Muhammad `Ali `Atif (Yemeni, age 19), acquitted during the trial in 1998;
> 4. Abu Hudayfa Abdallah Muhsin Salih al-Junaydi (Yemeni?), death sentence, commuted to 20 years;
> 5. Abu Hurayra Husayn Muhammad Salih (Tunisian), death sentence, commuted afterwards to 8 years;
> 6. Abu Nasir al-Awlaqi Sa`id al-Fayadi al-Malqab;
> 7. Abu `Abdallah Salim al-Fayadi al-Malqab;
> 8. `Ali `Awwad Ba-Rasayn;
> 9. `Ali Ahmad Haydara;
> 10. Rawsan Muhammad Salih;
> 11. Jalal al-Khudr;
> 12. Muhammad `Ali al-Humar;
> 13. Abu `Ubayd;
> 14. Salim al-Badawi; and
> 15. 3 Algerians and 2 Somalis.[80]

The names strongly indicate that IAAA was a group that had international connections. With Egyptians, Tunisians, Algerians and Somalis all participating in the kidnapping of tourists in Dec. 1998, IAAA was a global radical Muslim *jihadi* organization. However,

---

[77] This odd name, blasphemous to a radical Muslim (like the common name `Abd al-Rasul in Afghanistan that caused so many doctrinal difficulties), indicates the problems that exist between radical and popular Islam even with regards to names.
[78] "Yemen arrests four Aden Army members," *Arabic News* (March 3, 2003).
[79] E.g., "Aden-Abyan Islamic Army does not exist"—Abdennabi, *Arab News* (Feb. 8, 2004).
[80] *Al-Usbu`a* (Dec. 31, 1998).

the lack of prominence given to Yemenis also indicates that al-Mihdar did not have qualified people to work with, and that probably most of the Yemenis on the list who cannot be identified were simply drifters or various malcontents. According to the numbers listed by various Arabic news sources (most of which sound speculative) IAAA probably does not have more than 80-100 members.

The most intriguing element of IAAA is its international connections, especially to Abu Hamza al-Misri in London. Abu Hamza for most of his colorful career (between 1994 approximately and his expulsion from the Finsbury Park Mosque in London in 2003) has been the spokesperson for radical groups throughout the Arab world who did not otherwise have a voice. Abu Hamza not only had the personal connection with al-Mihdar, but he genuinely saw potential for an Islamic revolution in Yemen. The reasons for that were the comparatively untouched nature of the society (there is little Western presence), the high level of anti-Americanism, the high rate of population growth, and as Abu Mus`ab al-Suri notes, the level of weaponry available to the people. If a radical Islamic group could grow anywhere, it should be able to grow in the chaotic situation of Yemen. And if an Islamic state could be planted in Yemen, it would naturally be a threat to the Gulf States and to other American client states such as Ethiopia, perhaps Egypt and maybe even Israel. Such a level of strategy demonstrates the grandiose level of dreaming in which Abu Hamza engaged. However, it is worth noting that even after the collapse of the IAAA, Bin Ladin has continued to call for the "liberation" of Yemen.[81] Abu Hamza's involvement with IAAA was more than just spiritual; he also either sent or allowed his son Muhammad Mustafa Kamal and his stepson Muhsin Ghaylan to join.[82] The younger son was arrested by the Yemenis together with the other IAAA members in 1998, but released and returned to the U.K. on Jan. 28, 2002. The other intriguing association of the IAAA is that of Khalid al-Mihdar, one of the Sept. 11, 2001 highjackers (on American flight #77 that crashed into the Pentagon).[83] Unfortunately, other than the name similarity to the founder of IAAA, no further information about this connection is available.

> "Such a level of strategy demonstrates the grandiose level of dreaming in which Abu Hamza

3. <u>Operations associated with the Islamic Army of Aden Abyan</u>

IAAA was apparently founded in either 1996 or 1997. The similarity with the rising prominence of al-Qa`ida during those same years is striking. However, until its first declarations on May 19, 1998, its existence was shadowy. Presumably these first years were the recruitment phase of the new group. On Dec. 28, 1998 the IAAA kidnapped 16 tourists (12 Britons, 2 Americans and 2 Australians) to hold in exchange for the release of Islamic radicals held by the Yemeni government. (Kidnappings are hardly uncommon in Yemen, but most are tribal and designed to force concessions from the government on various issues of concern to the tribes.) According to the sources, eight of the members of IAAA stopped this tourist group at a roadblock, and after releasing the guides of the group to give their demands to the authorities, took them to a

---

[81] Bruce Lawrence (ed.), *Messages to the World: The Statements of Osama Bin Laden* (London: Verso, 2005), p. 183 (dated Feb. 11, 2003).
[82] Memri.org. "Inquiry and Analysis #72, "Abu Hamza al-Misri, Oct. 16, 2001.
[83] *The 9/11 Commission Report* (New York: W.W. Norton, 2004), p. 218.

hideout. The members of the IAAA killed two British women and one man, and then during a shootout with the authorities the following day another prisoner died from his injuries.[84] However, the leader of IAAA, al-Mihdar, was captured along with a number of others, and several were killed.

Interestingly enough, there had already been an arrest of the members of IAAA just a few days before this kidnapping. Six members of IAAA, all having British or French passports had been arrested on Dec. 23, 1998 (another four members of this group were arrested with the hostage takers). The arrested included: Shahid Butt (Pakistani, British nationality), Malik Nasir Harhara (Yemeni, British nationality), Ghulam Husayn (Pakistan, British nationality), Sarmad Ahmad (Pakistani, British nationality), Muhsin Ghaylan (Moroccan, British nationality, step-son of Abu Hamza), al-Jaza'iri (possible name: `Abd al-Rahman `Amr, Algerian, French nationality), Muhammad Mustafa Kamal (son of Abu Hamza), Shahzad Nabi (British nationality) and his cousin (?) Iyaz Husayn (British nationality), and Kamal `Ali Muhammad Saghir, known as Abu `Ali (Algerian nationality, but with a French passport). Two others, `Abdallah al-Junaydi (Yemeni) and Muhammad Ahmad (Tunisian) were also captured.[85]

They were carrying wool masks, military uniforms, implements designed to forge ID cards, GPS devices, phone systems, elements to aid in disguise and explosives. In retrospect it seems clear that the tourist kidnapping resulted in the premature revelation of the group that had intended to wait for a longer period before confronting the government or attacking foreign targets.

During the kidnapping of the tourists, Abu Hamza in London emerged as the principle contact man for IAAA. Al-Mihdar had phoned him after the kidnappings, and Abu Hamza's group, Ansar al-Shari`a (Supporters of Shari`a) issued a statement supporting IAAA on Dec. 30, 1998. But events had already moved beyond anything that Abu Hamza could control, and there is nothing in the statement except threats against foreigners in Yemen. Although the Yemeni government is held responsible for those who died in the attack, there is no sense of a political or religious program behind the group.[86] All-in-all, the operation was a complete failure for IAAA.

Initially the suicide attack on the destroyer U.S.S. *Cole* on Oct. 12, 2000 in the port of Aden was thought to have some connection to IAAA. In this prototypical naval suicide attack (for radical Muslims at least; the Liberation Tigers of Tamil-Eelam had been using them for some years in Sri Lanka) two attackers piloted a small fast inflatable boat close to the *Cole* and then detonated the explosives on board. Seventeen sailors and others were killed, and a substantial hole was blasted in the hull of the ship. Most probably the one who planned the attack was al-Harithi, the leader of al-Qa`ida in Yemen at the time (killed in 2002), while support was rendered by al-Nashiri, who was later captured by the United States in Oct. 2002. However, the close links between al-Qa`ida in Yemen and IAAA are revealed by reports that al-Harithi was killed in the company of IAAA men, four of whom were in his car when it was struck by a missile.[87]

---

[84] See the book of Mary Quin, *Kidnapped in Yemen* (Auckland, N.Z.: Random House, 2005).
[85] www.al-bab.com/yemen/hamza/suspects.htm.
[86] See "Yemen hostage communique No. 1" at www.al-bab.com/yemen/hamza/sos2.htm.
[87] http://www.cnsnews.com/ViewForeignBureaus.asp?Page=%5CForeignBureaus %5Carchive%5C200409%5CFOR20040930a.html.

The attack on the French oil tanker *Limburg* near the port of al-Daba in the city of al-Mukalla (in Hadramawt province close to Abyan) is tied to IAAA. This attack took place on Oct. 6, 2002, and has been interpreted as part of a string of attacks during that period (including the suicide attacks in Bali on Oct. 12, 2002) leading up to the U.S. invasion of Iraq. IAAA, under the leadership of `Abd al-Hakim Bazeeb, claimed the attack,[88] which like that on the *Cole* was carried out by a small skiff that exploded next to the tanker. However, because the *Limburg* was not anywhere near as heavily peopled as the *Cole*, only one person was killed (as a result of the fire that broke out) and 17 others injured. No other operations are attested for IAAA, but there are quite a number of rumors that still circulate in newspapers and information web-sites.

4. The End of the Islamic Army of Aden Abyan and its Importance

It is difficult to tell whether IAAA still exists. With Khalid `Abd al-Nabi's denials and no obvious operations for a number of years, it seems likely that the organization has simply collapsed. Probably more activist and radical elements have merged with al-Qa`ida in Yemen or been funneled off into martyrdom operations in Iraq.[89] It would make sense, then, that `Abd al-Nabi must have made a deal with the Yemeni government for amnesty in return for quiescence. Yet occasionally IAAA crops up in the news, such as on June 26, 2003, when six of them were apparently killed in the mountains of Hadramawt by Yemeni special forces.[90]

The importance of IAAA within Yemen was minimal. This was not a very major group and certainly posed no serious challenge to the regime. It is difficult to assess from the materials available how precisely they had planned on operating. There does not seem to have been any attempt on the part of IAAA to become a mass-movement or to recruit on a large scale. Although their operations embarrassed the Yemeni government (especially after Sept. 11, 2001 when it wanted to project the image to the outside world that it was fighting terror), they are not associated with any anti-governmental operations. Additionally, President Salih and his government demonstrated no great enthusiasm in investigating the elements that attacked the *U.S.S. Cole*, pardoned Khalid `Abd al-Nabi rather hastily, and presumably facilitated the prison break-out of Feb. 6, 2006.[91] All of these facts taken together suggest that the Yemenis would rather just ignore the problem or hope that it goes away if the militants are ignored and sidelined rather than confront them.

It also suggests that unlike other radical Muslim *jihadi* movements, IAAA has simply never targeted the government or made an attempt to promote violence against it.[92] All of its violence was directed against foreigners in Yemen, which, while devastating to the Yemeni economy and world prestige, was a far cry from the charges of *takfir* that so many radical Islamic groups level against their governments.[93] What then was

---

[88] See http://www.tkb.org/Incident.jsp?incID=9771.
[89] Moshe Marzuk, "Radical Islamic Organizations announce merger with al-Qa`ida" http://www.ict.org.il/spotlight/det.cfm?id=933.
[90] http://www.juancole.com/2003/06/reporters-on-ground-in-majar-al-kabir.html.
[91] http://www.yementimes.com/article.shtml?i=918&p=front&a=1.
[92] This is also the conclusion of Gregory Johnsen, "The Resiliency of Yemen's Aden-Abyan Islamic Army," at jamestown.org "Terrorism Monitor" 4:14 (July 13, 2006).
[93] For example, Algeria (GIA and GSPC) and Egypt (al-Gama`a al-Islamiyya, etc.).

the real goal of the IAAA? None of the operations that it carried out and took responsibility for were attacks upon the government; they all focused upon foreigners. Presumably the goal of the group was to rid Yemen of foreign influences. Why does al-Suri see it as one of the paradigmatic groups? Perhaps it is merely the fact that Yemen is central to the designs of al-Qa`ida—as so many of its members are Yemeni and the country is one that could conceivably fall under radical Muslim control. But it is equally possible that al-Suri mentions it because of his personal connections in Yemen as well.